AF487748

In order to protect the privacy of the people that have submitted stories some names and locations have been left out.

All stories were originally submitted by our audience to ghostsofamerica.com. The stories have been edited by us to better fit this book.

Compiled and edited by: Nina Lautner

Acknowledgements

We would like to thank all those who have submitted their stories to us. These are the people who make our site ghostsofamerica.com and this book possible.

We would also like to thank all the lost souls in these stories. We hope many of them will have found their way by the time this book is published.

CONTENTS

31. Haunted Home On HWY 46 - Deer Park, Wisconsin
32. Leave Her Alone - Fairmount, Illinois
33. Our White Farmhouse - Preemption, Illinois
34. Someone Was Angry - Gary, Indiana
35. His Hand Hurts - Adrian, Michigan
36. Ghosts Exist - Bay City, Michigan
37. They Are In The House - Pigeon, Michigan
38. Unwanted Entities - Sault Sainte Marie, Michigan
39. It Was Probably Floyd - Kingsley, Michigan
40. Weird Happenings - Wyoming, Michigan
41. Yoo-Hoo - Vestaburg, Michigan
42. That Man Right There - Petersburg, Michigan
43. Occupied - Carrollton, Ohio
44. A Girl Scout - Western Springs, Illinois
45. Rural Highland - Highland, Illinois
46. A Pure Sees Things - Bourbon, Indiana
47. An Old Southern Gentleman - Manchester, Michigan
48. The Women - Harrison Township, Michigan
49. Full Of Spirits - Flint, Michigan
50. Walking With Me - Gwinn, Michigan
51. He Was So Sorry - Seville, Ohio
52. A Gold Orb - Waterford, Michigan
53. Was It the Old Landlord? - Danville, Illinois
54. Weeping Spirit - Harrison Township, Michigan
55. Apartment 3 - Edgerton, Wisconsin
56. She Came Home With Me - Carpentersville, Illinois
57. Evil Spirit - Portsmouth, Ohio
58. The 700 Block - Greensburg, Indiana
59. Tragedy After Tragedy - Brighton, Michigan
60. The Other Residents - Stevens Point, Wisconsin
61. Black Mass - Chicago, Illinois

1.

Is This A Gift?
Maroa, Illinois

Ever since I was a kid I could see things, but I have never really thought about it much. However, as I got older, these things I would see became scarier and scarier. I would see shadows and faces looking at me. I saw people standing in my room only to cover my face, and these apparitions just vanished. In March 2001 I saw something that scared me. I was just lying in my bed, and I saw this face on my ceiling smiled. Then it frowned, but I thought nothing of it.

A few weeks later on March 3rd, 2001 we lost my mom. She passed away. This was when I knew exactly what it was. It was someone telling me everything was okay, but sadness would be approaching. On March 3rd, 2001 after my mom passed I went to sleep at a home on E Watson Street in Forrest, IL. I fell asleep on the chair. I woke up about two the next morning. Something really frightened me. As I looked up, I could see a huge ball or orb coming towards me. The closer it got, the brighter it got. As it entered the living room, the orb of light changed and formed a human figure like angel wings, but there was no face. It was tall with a white robe.

As this tall figure came near me, I saw a hand come out, and it was put on mine which calmed me down. I
4

then saw this figure go into my dad's room. My dad woke up the next morning and looked at me. He said "Bobby, you're not going to believe what happened to me last night, but someone whispered in my ear "thank you for what you did for me". This was when I knew that I had a gift.

 I'm still trying to understand it but still continue to see things to this day. I now live in a small town, and the building I live in I do believe is haunted. I woke up one night. It was really cold, and I happened to look over at my bedroom door and saw a man in his early 20s standing there. He dressed in a US Air Force uniform. I went to talk to this man, and I turned my head for just a second. Then the man was gone. Is this a gift, or am I just seeing things?

Submitted by Bob, Maroa, Illinois

. . . .

2.
Not Elaine
French Lick, Indiana

My wife and I stayed one night in a hotel on the 4th floor around four years ago in May 2014. We were unfamiliar with the hotel and its reputation. A friend gave us the trip as a getaway golf outing. That night I awoke in the middle of the night (around 1 or 2 a.m.) and heard sobbing coming from the bathroom. I figured it was Elaine, but I couldn't guess why. After a few minutes of this she reached up to the toilet stool handle and began jiggling it. Metal on porcelain makes a very distinctive sound. The room was semi-dark, the bathroom darker, and the water-closet pitch dark.

I got up and went to the bathroom to ask what was wrong. I looked around the corner to the water-closet and spoke "Elaine?" There was no response. The sobs and noise had stopped when I got out of bed. I went back to bed and slowly reached across the mattress and found that my wife was still sleeping on the bed. I didn't get back up. I decided that I am a Christian and that if something was to happen, I was confident that all would be okay. Then I went back to sleep until morning. I have no explanation.

Submitted by Ed, French Lick, Indiana
. . . .

3.
The Blue Boy And A Dark Spirit
Hubbardston, Michigan

I lived for five years in an old house in Hubbardston. There were a few off occurrences that happened in those five years. One night about a year after moving in my now ex-wife woke in the middle of the night, looked out of the windows facing out neighbors yard, and she explained that she saw a small boy approximately eight to ten years old crawling on his hands and knees towards the neighbor's back yard. She said he was bathed in blue light and disappeared when she looked away.

A short time later while renovating the master bedroom we found some family pictures that belonged to the family that built and lived in the house before us. My ex told me that she recognized the boy in some of the pictures as the boy in blue. We spoke to our elderly neighbor about the pictures without asking about the boy in blue. She saw the pictures and described how the boy was born with a heart condition and would visit her late husband when he would be gardening in the back yard. She added that since the boy had a hole in his heart he was not able to walk and would crawl everywhere. She told us that the boy didn't live past twelve. The boy passed in the late 1950s to early 1960s. She added that he had poor circulation and had a touch of blue to his lips.

My family was just starting out when I moved to the house. My son was only a month old when we closed. When he was about 16 months old a family friend was visiting. She claimed to be sensitive to some supernatural things. She said that she did not want to alarm us, but there was a force in the house that wanted to do harm to our son. I faked concern and thanked the friend for her warning. We changed the subject, and I didn't give it much thought.

This next incident happened about a month later.

There were two bedrooms upstairs one for my ex and me and the other for our young son. One day I set my son down for a nap in his crib. I shut the door to his room, walked down stairs, and shut the door at the bottom of the stairs. We had other friends over. After about ten minutes of visiting we heard a series of knocks at the door at the bottom of the stairs. I slowly opened the door and found my son standing at the bottom of the stairs.

My son was a fat baby and only started walking two months earlier. He was too short to reach the door knob to his bedroom and had never crawled on stairs. It was another three months before he was able to crawl out of crib on his own. Needless to say, both bedrooms were moved downstairs that very day!

Another strange occurrence happened about three years after moving in. We had an orange tiger cat in the house. One day after getting home he was nowhere to be found. After a search of the house I found him dead lying on the floor in my son's old upstairs bedroom. He was fairly young, maybe two years old at the most. I buried him out back. I figured he caught rabies or something and didn't think much about it.

A few months before we moved out, my ex and I were having trouble. We were having problems with the marriage and with finances. We had a few arguments but nothing that had become overly loud or close to physically violent. One night a regular disagreement turned into a full on shouting match. We were in each other faces screaming, crying, and name calling. The argument devolved into us not being able to find a resolution. I refused to sleep in the bed with her. I exclaimed that I was going to sleep in the upstairs bedroom on the guest bed.

The door to that bedroom and my son's old room were directly across from each other. The short hall leading to the stairs was all that separated the rooms. A few moments after I lay on the bed I heard a strange noise in the other bedroom. I looked through the open doorway and didn't see anything. The only things in the room were a toddler bed frame and an empty dresser.

I turned and faced away from the room and tried to get comfortable. I tried to calm down from the argument I just left downstairs. A few moments later I heard a more violent noise from the other bedroom. The noises continued to get louder and louder. It sounded as if someone was in the room and was throwing things around trying to break everything. I was afraid to turn my head toward the open doorway. I was not sure of what I would have seen.

Finally after what was a minute but seemed like forever I worked up the nerve to make a run for the stairway. The noises continued. I spun around springing of for the bed and sprinting for the door. As I made it into the hallway, I looked into the room. Nothing was out of place although the sounds continued. They did not stop until I made it to the bottom of the stairs. Although I was scared I was still holding grudge against my ex. I didn't mention what had just happened and slept on the couch.

Later the next day we talked about the argument. Neither of us could remember what started the fight, what we were fighting about, or what made us both so mad. The only thing she heard while I was upstairs was me running down the stairs. She did notice that I came downstairs and walked into the living room. Her emotions were running high, and she lay awake for a long while that night.

We lost the house to foreclosure within a year and moved. I really have not encountered anything like that since. I joined a ghost hunting group years later and had some strange experiences but nothing like what I encountered in that house.

Looking back, I think there were two entities living in that house. The blue boy and another much darker spirit. This is only a feeling though.

Submitted by Andy, Hubbardston, Michigan

. . . .

4.
The Last Meal
Paxton, Indiana

During the depression my grandmother Dora lived in Paxton. There was an old lady who was on her last leg, and grandma moved her in to take care of her in her final days. The doctor came to check on her and told grandma she didn't have long and just make her happy. She asked the old lady what she would like to eat. She wanted just some chicken soup. They had no chickens and couldn't afford to buy one, so she went to those in town who did have chickens and asked for one, so she could give the old lady what was likely her final meal. Nobody would help. They said they were not about to waste a chicken on someone who was going to die anyway. That was the last place she went. She closed the gate and was walking down the road and heard a cluck behind her.

She turned and saw one of the birds had followed her. Somehow it got out of the yard. She shooed it back in, closed the gate, and walked on. Then again the same thing. The third time she looked around she didn't see anyone, so she reached down the chicken's neck. She took it home and made the old lady her chicken soup. She died that night. When the funeral was held everyone was there with their flowers, and all so broken up. They all took turns laying their flowers on the casket. My grandma was about to do so too, and out of nowhere a big gust of wind came up and blew them all off. They tried again. All the flowers were blown off. They didn't have the guts to try it a third time. Grandma went up, laid the flower on the casket, and there was no breeze. My mother was about fourteen and saw this herself.

Submitted by Damond, Paxton, Indiana

. . . .

5.
Wandering Soul
New Buffalo, Michigan

I lived in a haunted house on Laporte Road in New Buffalo. I was a teenager when we moved in and left when I was 21. You couldn't pay me to stay the night by myself. It was probably built in the early 1900s, and I was told it had been a doctor's office. It was haunted by a lady in a blue dress who would swish by you.

The house had a big room upstairs, and the lady ghost would come gliding down the stairs. My dad would ask her to have a cup of coffee with him. One time I was home by myself, and someone turned the stereo on full blast in the back bedroom. Then they kept changing the stations. I also heard old fashion music coming from the bedroom.

My mother heard a lady crying, but she put a Jesus picture up with a night light, and the crying stopped. I was always fascinated by the house. My mother loved the house, but my dad hated it, and he ended up dying in it. It was haunted for sure.

The house isn't there anymore. All that's left is the big Christmas tree. They built a McDonald's and a hotel on the land that went with the house. The place where the house was is just an empty spot. It is strange nothing was built there. I wonder if the lady in the blue dress went to McDonald's or the hotel. She was harmless, not really scary, just a poor lost wandering soul.

Submitted by Esther, New Buffalo, Michigan

. . . .

6.
You Are Not Wanted
Muskegon, Michigan

I work for a property management company here in
Muskegon. I show a lot of our properties to potential
renters. We have houses all over the county and had a
few that just don't feel right. Sometimes it feels like
someone is watching you. I have even heard footsteps
a few times after everyone has left.

There are two places that I wouldn't mind ever going to
again. We have a pretty decent sized home on 6th
Street near Muskegon High School that another
employee told me that she hates showing it and think
that it's haunted.

Forgetting her fears about it, I showed it to a group of
people that had a few children with them. At that time
I had only been on the main floor of the home and was
curious of what the upstairs looked like. Half way up
the stairs, I started to feel sick. I got up there, and I had
to quickly look around because my dizziness got
worse. I felt as if I was going to throw up or pass out.
As I walked down the stairs to the main level, I felt a
hand on my back try to push me, and I almost tumbled
down the stairs but caught myself on the railing.

Wanting to get out of there but still have people
looking around, I stood by the front door. As I was

standing there, I was watching this kid about nine to ten walking up the stairs, stopped, and turned around to answer his grandmother's call for him. It looked like something pushed him and about to trip down a couple of steps. He looked around like he might have thought it was his brother and saw no one there; he looked at me with the biggest fearful eyes, probably similar to the ones that I had just moments before. When I finally got everyone out of there, I never got out of house so quickly.

I went to work the next day and told my co-worker what happened. She told me that is exactly what happened to her when she was there last. She felt as if someone was trying to push her down the stair and felt sick upstairs. It's a beautiful home and got rented rather quickly (fortunate for me,) and I always wonder if the tenants had any issues. I don't want to sound crazy, so of course I would never ask them. They have been there quite awhile now, so things must be fine.

Another house that's located near the high school on Mason that has been split into two apartments is one of the most awful and uncomfortable places I have ever been. While upgrading the property the maintenance men would say that it was haunted and hated working there. They said that they would hear rustling and music coming from upstairs. They would feel like a large man would be standing behind them. When they turned around nothing would be there. I went in there to check it out one day, and I got the worse pain in my chest. There was a smell I can't describe. I felt like I was not wanted in there, and I didn't want to be in there.

We put alarm systems in our empty properties, and one day the motion sensor inside the home kept going off, but none of the other sensors on the doors or windows were. We thought maybe it was faulty. We checked it out, and it seemed fine, so we moved it to another area of the property, and it never went off again. When I showed the property I would stand outside. I would only go in to disarm the alarm and unlock it. That one as well was rented now, both upstairs and down.

Submitted by R, Muskegon, Michigan

. . . .

7.
They Are Welcome To Stay
Algonquin, Illinois

I live on the Fox River. It's more considered Barrington Hills out here. My house is not too old, and the man who built it is still living. I will start with what I have seen outside. I drove down 25 late one night. I got to the part where it is farm fields. I looked out to the right and saw an old time lantern moving through the field. I really don't think they use the old lanterns anymore. It was a lantern with a candle because I could see the candle flickering. I also have seen strange mists and orbs while sitting outside at night. They just come out of nowhere and move on.

Now my house, let me explain it first. We have a separate garage with a suite above the garage, and the house has three levels, and you can get outside from all 3 levels. When we first moved in it needed a complete remodel, so we lived in the downstairs area for awhile. At night my father, who is a complete skeptic on anything paranormal, would hear light footsteps walking above us. He even went up a few times to see if someone broke in, but no one was up there. It takes a lot to spook my father, and this spooked him. My daughter and I often hear people upstairs when no one is home too. We call up there only to hear no response.

One time I was out in the garage. I heard someone knock on the door above me to the suite, then open the door, but I didn't hear any footsteps up to the door. There were no footsteps into the suite, nothing. I ran outside saying "I'm going to call the police!" Only to find the door wide open, and no one was there. If it was a person, they had to have some ninja skills to avoid me seeing them running away. I looked everywhere, and there was no one.

Then my boyfriend moved in. He has heard the footsteps above us, and one night he watched a light turn off in front of him. Thinking the bulb burnt out, he found out the bulb was fine, but the switch got turned off. I looked up history of this area. I know there were at one time Native Americans here, and it was farmland for awhile. I also found that there was a camp directly across the river from me at one point, and three boys drowned in the river somewhere near my house, before I moved out this way. I don't know if any of that has to do with who walks around at night above us, but it's interesting to read about. Nothing here has been harmful, so I have no problems with them, and they are welcome to stay.

Submitted by Anonymous, Algonquin, Illinois

. . . .

8.
In The Attic
Berwyn, Illinois

I grew up in a house on S. Highland Avenue. We had something unidentifiable living in the house, living in the basement and attic. My oldest brother owned it from 1962 until he sold it in 1983 or 1984. It was a clear presence without form. I remember living in the attic dormitory. It wasn't frightening until after dark. The presence arrived in the dark. Some nights I left the light on all night long. I never wanted to be in the basement after dark alone either. The presence was there, too.

I asked my oldest niece who lived in the house and used the attic dormitory as a play room. She agreed that after dark the attic and basement were off limits. I can't find any records of murders or other deaths that occurred in the house prior to my own father's death in 1982. Dad died at 7 p.m. on November 12th, 1982 in the west bedroom of the hall off the dining room. His death postdated the haunting.

However, interestingly, the day he died, he claimed to see his mother "walking down the street letting down her long brown hair. " Her name was Anna Clara. She died in 1918 of cancer and is buried at Rose Hill Cemetery in Chicago. Mom and dad are buried at Elm Lawn in Elmhurst. It is common for Christians to see departed loved ones the day they die. Mom and I saw the physical manifestation one night separately. For me he entered my room via the attic portion of the attic/dormitory through the closet. He sat on my bed, and I quickly covered my head never to see him again. Mom saw him the same night at the foot of her bed. To both of us he appeared as a blue sequined man with a blue top hat.

I lived there 1970-1983 and never felt comfortable after dark. I still experience an occasional nightmare when I am back at the house. It always takes fervent prayer to God and an assist from holy guardian angels or the Holy Ghost to end the nightmare, so it must be a demonic presence. Though I live about two hours away, I still occasionally travel to Berwyn to walk past the house. As horrifying as the dreams are, the house still draws me.

Submitted by Ira, Berwyn, Illinois

. . . .

9.

It Didn't Want Us

Blanchard, Michigan

In December of 2015 we came very close to purchasing the old home next to Mill Pond. We immediately fell in love with the house and property, and at $48,000 it seemed like a steal although there was a lot of work to be done. We were not worried because we are builders by trade and have taken on extensive remodeling projects in the past. We felt it would be a nice place to raise our young boys. We put in an offer which was accepted by HUD and were ready to cut a check. We revisited the house a couple more times that December to discuss the restoration plan.

The second morning my husband slipped and landed flat on his back at the house. Minutes later my 9-year-old son slipped and fell there as well. I tried to brush the eerie feeling off but took the falls almost as a warning. It was early in the morning on the second visit, and we were the only people there that day. The home didn't have heat, and there was frost on the glass windows on the enclosed front porch. When I looked out I distinctly saw a handprint melted through the ice from the inside as if someone was looking out. No one else had been on the porch, and my kids were too short to have made the mark.

By our third visit I could no longer bring myself to get out of the car when we were there. I just remember getting a creepy feeling that the house didn't want us as the new owners. I jokingly say that house could have killed us if we tried to restore it, but I am only partially kidding. We withdrew our offer just after. I have been through Blanchard a few times and think the new owners are doing an amazing job on the remodel. The new owner's post does confirm my feelings, and I just wanted her to know she is not alone. We felt it too!

Submitted by Carrie, Blanchard, Michigan

. . . .

10.
Housekeeping Ghost
Amelia, Ohio

My mother and I moved to Amelia in 1992 after my parents decided to divorce. I was 12 at the time. My mother chose this area because it was close to her twin sister who lived in East Fork State Park. We moved into an apartment in what is now called the Oakmont Flats. We moved into Building 7, Apartment 2.

During the moving process we had small boxes stacked to the ceiling. My mother and I left to get dinner. When we came back the top four boxes were down on the ground, and our dog wanted out of that house. He did not want to come back in either. My mother and I figured the boxes must have fallen.

After we had settled in I woke up one night to hear the dining room closet slam shut. My mother was sleeping, and I could hear her snoring. I thought it was just the neighbors. The next night I had left my closet door open on one side. These were sliding doors. I heard the door slam shut. I left my room and slept on the sofa instead. There were a few more nights of this. My mother noticed it too, so we decided that the ghost must want us to keep the doors shut, so we complied.

One day after running errands my mother placed some air freshener under the kitchen sink. The next morning the air freshener was in the bathroom. We moved it back, and again we would find it back in the bathroom. My mother and I joked that the ghost didn't like farts, so we kept the air freshener in the bathroom. The ghost we felt was friendly but just liked the house a certain way. We learned to put dishes in the dishwasher, air freshener in the bathroom, closet doors closed and vacuum cleaner in the hall closet.

A few months later a friend and her daughter came to stay with us for a few weeks. We told her about our house keeping ghost, and she didn't believe us. She decided one night to leave dishes in the sink, to leave the closet doors open, move the air freshener and leave the vacuum cleaner in my room. She was staying in my room while I slept on the sofa. We were woken up by a loud bang coming from the bathroom. My mother, her friend, and I walked in to the bathroom to find the bathroom completely destroyed. Towels were pulled from the cabinet and were thrown about. All the toiletries that normally sit on the counter were in the sink. The air freshener was on the counter, and the shampoo that was normally in the bath tub was in the sink as well.

I also noticed all the closet doors were closed, the vacuum in its usual spot, and the dishes on the floor. The sound of breaking glass was what woke us up. Written on the mirror was the word STOP. It was not in anyone's handwriting. I told my mother's friend to

26

stop teasing the ghost. My mother told her the same thing. She left a few days later as the activity escalated, and she was the target.

After this for about a year things were fine. We would occasionally have occurrences such as closet doors closing or stuff being moved. We lived in relative peace with this ghost until one day in December.

My mother, her twin sister, and a friend of theirs decided to play with a Ouija board. They said they wanted to talk to our house keeping ghost. I told them that it was a bad idea and chose to stay the night at a friend's house. The next night I was home, and it would be the worst night of my life.

I got woken up by a strange voice calling my name. I didn't see anyone and thought my mother must have been talking in her sleep again. The walls were paper thin in that apartment. I rolled over and tried to go back to sleep. I felt something grab the foot of my bed. I then felt the lower part of my bed rise up and slam down. My head hit the wall. It happened several more times. Then it just stopped. I sat up in bed scared but unwilling to call out to my mother. I learned a hard lesson early in life not doing that.

I tried to get up to turn on the light but felt something push me back. Thinking I lost my balance, I tried again. This time I pushed back onto the bed and felt something grab my throat. I felt it pushing me down, and when I reached for what was grabbing my throat there was nothing there. I started to recite the Lord's Prayer. It stopped.

The next morning I found bruises on my chest and neck. I also found three scratches on my back. I told no one fearing they would think I was crazy. The attacks would happen every couple of months. Even when we moved the attacks would continue and continued for a couple of years. They stopped when I found the Ouija board and destroyed the board.

The other odd thing about the apartment complex was the maintenance shop. It was the original main office and is located in the back by building #14. There is an old pool there that is filled in. One night while walking my dog, I saw a teenage girl about my age hanging out by the maintenance shop. Thinking it was someone new, I went up to talk with her. As I approached her, I saw her run towards the old pool and disappear. It turned out she was the spirit of a teenage girl who jumped the fence one night. She hit her head and drowned in the pool.

Submitted by Jenn, Amelia, Ohio

. . . .

11.
Offices in 216
River Falls, Wisconsin

In 1998 I was the editor of the student newspaper based in South Hall. One Wednesday night as we were working on the paper, two of my staff were in the hallway outside our offices in 216 and noticed what they thought was a fellow section editor quietly walking up the stairs to the abandoned/locked-off third floor.

They called her name, only to be shocked as the person they thought they were looking at on the stairs, answered their call from behind them. The figure on the stairs then glided silently up the stairs and vanished. The next I knew my staff was screaming and running back into the office, saying they had just seen a ghost.

We all investigated, walked-up the darkened stairs to third floor, and checked that the door. The floor was indeed padlocked (it was). The stairwells always felt as if you were sharing the space with something, the closed spaces in the building the same.

That was the only sighting, but in my four years in that building, you heard and saw all kinds of things that never made sense. At night, late at night, you could hear what sounded like kids running and balls rolling on the floor past the office or above on the third floor. The building had been a teacher's college, and all the doorknobs were at a child's height, so the sounds made an eerie sort of sense.

Walking back home after late nights at the paper, you'd see lights on up on the disused abandoned third floor. Shadows flit across windows when you knew there was no reason for anyone to be up there. Later, checking with campus security, they'd say nobody had been on the floor and that, yes, they saw the lights too.

There was a period of time when South Hall was threatened with being demolished, and many of us took up the cause to write for its saving and restoration. I always felt that the building thanked me for that, as I never felt threatened in the building no matter where I went. I don't think I'm attuned to spirits, but I definitely felt something in that building.

I've gone back since, and in my opinion the reuse/restoration of the last decade ruined the building's character and, I think, its spirit. The feeling I had in walking the halls and in the closed dark spaces in the classrooms and in our old offices in 216 was gone.

Maybe whatever was there has moved on. Maybe all I ever felt was the effects of sleep-deprivation, my staff thinking the ghost they saw was mere hallucinating from Jolt cola, or maybe something wanted to tell us a story?

Submitted by Michael, River Falls, Wisconsin

. . . .

12.
Still Happening
Bedford, Indiana

I live next to the Fayetteville Store, which is a gas station in the heart of the community. Before the 1990s, a house sat in between my house and the store, which burned down about thirty years ago. The foundation and the backyard steps still remain, however. Fortunately, the inhabitants were not fatally injured directly because of the fire.

About two months later one of the two was walking in my front yard to the church. They collapsed and died. To make things a little more eerie for us, the previous owners of my home had a son who died just before we bought our house. We were not aware of this until two weeks later, when the father had told us what had happened. His son died in what is now my bedroom.

In about 2008 I began to have these weird dreams where these people would talk to me and jump out of the weirdest places. This would always happen to me right before I am sighting something. The next morning I took my shower just before I was going to church. When I was getting out I saw this ghostly looking man. He appeared to be about twenty years old, gazing right at me through the window. He was transparent and had really short hair.

I didn't have another dream like that until March 8th, 2009 just before an EF3 tornado struck the area, wiping homes clean off of their foundations. Right after we received the call, the same man was staring at me in the same exact location. I asked my parents and siblings if they had seen anything like this. They said that they had no idea what I was talking about.

Around Christmastime in 2009 I heard footsteps late at night. I made out this older man who was at my front door. About three or four seconds later he let out a moan and collapsed and vanished. On May 24th, 2011 I had the same dream that I had three times before. The next day, five minutes before another EF3 tornado touched down, I saw the same 20-year-old man who looked like he had not aged since the last time I saw him in 2009. I had the pastor of my church pray over my house, yet these occurrences still happen. The last time this happened was two years ago, and I doubt it will happen again. Still, it was creepy to go through all of this.

Submitted by Benjamin, Bedford, Indiana

. . . .

13.
Scent Of Fall
Austin, Indiana

My spouse and I bought a home built in the 70s, which had been abandoned for around four years. I had been told that the former owners had separated, and the wife had died (whether in the home or not I do not know). Over the years apparently there had been several squatters who had stayed in the house. The house was vandalized and trashed. We gathered up enough syringes to fill a 5-gallon bucket.

We ended up pretty much rebuilding the entire house inside with new wiring, plumbing, about 90% new drywall, new subfloors and flooring, new cabinets, and bath fixtures. After moving into the house my husband and I have both seen and felt the presence of "something" usually either in the hallway of the main floor or in the peripheral vision in the doorway of the living room. Small objects tend to disappear and are found in places that have no explanation as to why they would be there.

One day I was taking clothes out of totes as we were just moving in. I was sorting the clothing and was stacking it on the bed. I turned away toward the tote I was working out of and turned back to see one of the articles of clothing fall off the bed onto the floor. Not a big deal right? Not so fast. The sweatshirt landed on the floor UNDER THE BED by about a foot from the edge of the bed. This happened several times with different articles. I would literally watch them come off the bed and go under the bed. (The bed is an antique iron bed which sits fairly high off the floor).

After watching this, intrigued, I finally said out loud, "look, I don't care if you are here, I don't care if you stay but don't make me keep bending over this way. My back hurts. " It didn't happen again that day and has only happened a hand full of times in the next two years, but never falling beneath the bed. The sound of footsteps is either in the hallway of the main floor going up the stairs to the second floor, or on the second floor while we are downstairs. It happens so frequently we barely notice anymore. Our dogs will growl and/or bark for no reason. Light bulbs have a very short life span before burning out, and anything battery operated goes through batteries so quickly that I tend to just not replace them.

My family is concerned. They say that we have had "bad luck" since moving there. We have lost several family members (none live with us and only one ever visited the home). We have had two pets pass away. I feel like that is a bit of a stretch though to link that to the house. We purchased the house during the summer, and shortly after purchasing it I would smell a strong scent in the dining room area. It would come and go. It smelled like a caramel coffee or candle. It was the scent you would normally associate with fall. I had none of these in the house. We have also heard loud noises such as a very heavy object falling and been unable to find anything out of place.

Submitted by Cathy, Austin, Indiana

. . . .

14.
She's By The Well
Jasper, Indiana

There's an old house in Jasper. It's on the corner of 3rd and Clay. It's been abandoned since the 60s. The house was built around the turn of the century for an elderly woman. The back yard had its own well with very fancy brick work around the well and into the yard and favorite place for the neighborhood kids to play. I was told one day an accident happened with one of the kids playing around the well. No one knows exactly what happened, but the well was shut and covered over with dirt, and the elderly woman was moved from the house she loved and moved to a nursing home.

It fell into disrepair as she refused to sell her little house. Her children asked one of the neighbor kids now grown to buy the place, and it was sold. Soon after the woman died, but her old neighbors would always tell of seeing her standing by the well at her little house long after she had died.

You can take a meter there, and it will indicate a presence always by the well. On some occasions there will be another moving around the back as if a kid in play. The house is still there. If you look, you can see the top of the filled well and the brick in the backyard. I have seen on three occasions what looks like a faded woman in an old dress, but it's kind of fades in and out not really a glow, not really solid, and more like a faded life size picture. Sometimes it is like a glow from the well only seen on darkest nights or early morning.

Submitted by Parker, Jasper, Indiana

. . . .

15.
Many Died Here
Howell, Michigan

I live on S. Elm Street in downtown. I have lived here for nine years, and my wife has been here for fifteen years. Our home definitely has activity. One day we came home from the lake down the street, and we found an elderly lady sitting on our porch. I greeted her, and she asked if we lived there and that she had some "records" that should stay with the home. This home was relocated from Wetmore Street where the train station is now located.

It was built in the 1800s and moved around 1924. She had photos going back to the homes original location and up to its current when she last visited the home in 1992. It was 2016 when we met. She had pictures and stories, all fascinating, but we learned that several people had died here over the years and that funerals were routinely held in our parlor. Before we knew of these details we had experienced many strange occurrences. However, they have all been either benign or even protective. One example is when I was sitting in our barn (it's one of the only homes in Howell city limits with a barn.) I had the garage doors all closed because it was cold and rainy. I was using my smoker, which I had setup in the driveway about 40' from the barn.

At about 3:30 am while I was flipping through a magazine, somebody started pounding on my sheet metal garage doors. The noise was loud and scared the hell out of me. My heart was racing, and I froze. Then it happened again. This time I ran up to the door and slung it open, (this door was not equipped with an opener) and there was nobody there. My driveway is over 100' long and there was no way that a prankster could have disappeared before I opened the door. My smoker was engulfed in flames. The thermostat had failed. I was clearly being alerted to this.

Weeks later I was awakened on the couch about 1:30 am and had a strange sense to go upstairs where my wife and daughter were sleeping. Climbing the stairs, I smelled smoke. There was a fire in the wall of the bedroom where they were sleeping, caused by a defective electrical outlet. Again, I was clearly alerted as I sleep like a rock. One night I was eating some food at the dining room table, and an old dried maple leaf landed on my plate. It fell from the ceiling from out of nowhere. It was harmless but interesting.

I have a bulldog that is usually very quiet but often barks at dark corners near the ceilings of certain rooms. My grandfather committed suicide in Germany in 1942. He was connected to the SS. He was a conductor and composer and rubbed elbows frequently with some of the wars most infamous and sinister people. Once he realized the horrors that were being committed to the Jews, he wanted to leave but could not. He hanged himself under an old cuckoo clock. Many years later I got this clock from my grandmother's estate; it was her father who took his life.

I had the clock restored and hung it in my kitchen. Bad idea. We had enormous amounts of paranormal activity almost immediately after I hung it, which was odd because my grandmother had it for 45 years in her home and never had a problem. After about two weeks, my entire family and I were eating dinner in our dining room, which is connected to the kitchen where the clock was hanging. CRASH! I ran in to see what had happened and found the clock had been smashed against its opposing wall, about fifteen feet away. It hit with so much force that it damaged the plaster wall. The clock was in fifty pieces. We were stunned, and our kids were scared to death.

It turns out; the old lady that visited us explained that one of the people that had lived and died there was a captain stationed in Germany in WW2. He came home paralyzed from a Nazi bullet to his back. He died here in our dining room on a gurney in the 1950s. The lady explained that if his ghost was in our home, he would not take kindly to that German artifact being in the home. The clock has been stored, in pieces, ever since. I have many more stories of occurrences that are too numerous to mention here.

We have things from somebody lying on the bed with my wife and I to handprints on fogged glass. It was of a hand that fits nobody's here. We heard creaking floors and just strange anomalies in general. Just last week my six-year-daughter thanked me for stroking her back as she slept. It wasn't me or my wife, and our sons were all away from home that night. She also told us of a strange boy that "blocked the stairs. " When pressed, she said that she used to be afraid, but not anymore because the boy seemed sad and couldn't talk. She isn't remotely concerned. In general, we don't feel intimidated or nervous and still love this charming old home. One last thing to point out is the activity definitely increases substantially every fall.

Submitted by Sean, Howell, Michigan

. . . .

16.
They Liked Us
Howell, Michigan

I used to own a house off W. Washington Street. I believe it was haunted but by spirits that liked us. When we first bought it, we did a lot of interior cosmetic stuff. We went to leave out of the back door and off the deck. My husband turned off all the lights to the house, so it was very dark. I misremembered how many steps were on the deck and fell forward. The sidewalk widened to the length of the steps then narrowed to a normal size. I somehow fell sideways into the grass. I have no idea how I didn't fall face-first on the concrete.

I also was home alone one day and decided to repaint the bathroom. I was scared of the basement because it was a field stone foundation (cinder block in part), so I was talking out loud. I couldn't find an edger or the pads to it. I took everything out of our painting supply tub, muttering that it had to be there somewhere. I just took a paint brush instead and declared that I would attempt to free-hand it. When I got upstairs, I realized I forgot a paint stirrer. I went back downstairs, and there was one edger and two pads laying out on top on the box like they had been left for me. I just said "thank you" and ran upstairs.

Another time I was coming home from work, and in my side mirror I saw a tall young man with red hair walking swiftly behind my car towards my neighbor's house. There's a tall wooden fence between our yards there, so there's no way a person would walk briskly right into the fence. I called out my husband's name, but I knew it wasn't him. He was inside on the couch.

Submitted by CM, Howell, Michigan

. . . .

17.
In Front Of The Elevator
Manistee, Michigan

I was staying at the Little River Casino Resort in Manistee, MI. I have gone there plenty of times before but never experienced a ghost sighting until last night. I was there with my mom and a couple of her friends. We got a room and went to the Gary Allan concert for my birthday. I left the concert and went back to the room. I waited till the concert was over to meet my mom and her friends downstairs.

We sat by the fire pit for a while then went to my mom's car to grab something she forgot. We all came back in, and I decided to go to the room while they went and got food. On my way back up to the room I went on the wrong elevator and ended up on floor 2, so I figured I'd walk to the other elevator on the other side of the hotel to see if it went up two more floors. (Our room was on the fourth floor.)

When I got about a third of the way there I stopped in my tracks and couldn't help but stare in shock. I walked a little further to make sure I wasn't delusional because I have glasses and wasn't wearing them at this time. As I got closer my heart started beating out of my chest, at the end of this hallway was a little girl with her back facing the elevator and staring at the chair that's across from the elevator. I was in complete disbelief. She just stood there hollow looking .I could see the shape of her upper body but her legs faint.

I turned around and walked away as fast as I could with every few steps looking back to make sure she didn't notice me. I then got on my phone and started calling my mom and her friends. None of them answered. I kept calling and finally got a call back from one of her friends. My voice was so shaky; she could hardly understand me. I proceeded to tell her I didn't know what elevator to take to get back to the room.

I didn't say anything about what I saw as I assumed she would think I was crazy. I got back to the room, and they showed up with food and drinks about thirty minutes later. I felt safer in my room but was still scared to be alone. We all ended up going to sleep about an hour later, and I didn't have another paranormal experience.

Submitted by Cierra, Manistee, Michigan

. . . .

18.
He Likes Music
Ashville, Ohio

One of the banks in Ashville, Ohio is definitely haunted. The spirit that lurks this building is pure evil. My first time ever being in this building was when I was with a coworker, and I could feel the presence of something right away. We had to go upstairs to work, and the only way up was the elevator. She is claustrophobic and insisted on riding the elevator up alone. I waited on the first floor for the elevator to return, and while waiting something flipped my ponytail. Once upstairs, I went into a conference room to begin working. Then I started coughing uncontrollably for no reason. I didn't stop coughing until I returned to the first floor.

Three days later I returned to the same building for work, but this time I was alone. I tried to return to the second floor but had such an overwhelming feeling of something being there; I couldn't go upstairs. I started working downstairs and turned some music on through my cell phone. The song barely started playing, and then it stopped. I checked my phone and had a great signal, but it showed the music was paused. I pressed play again, and the same thing happened again, so I said aloud "I'm sorry. You don't like that song. Why don't you choose one you like?" My music started to skip through songs and finally stopped on one I assume the spirit liked. In less than an hour my fully charged cell phone was now in the red and ready to die. I turned the music off. While working I glanced over to the security camera live feed and caught an image of a fuzzy black figure.

While talking to other coworkers about this, they admitted to similar experiences. Their experiences include music being advanced to a different song or a song repeating itself over and over. In the same conference room that I could not stop coughing another coworker that had no clue this had happened admitted she saw a dark figure sitting in (that same room). Another coworker said she felt like she was being strangled in the elevator and then said the same song was playing over and over on her phone. I've just started researching the building, but so far I've found nothing.

Submitted by Karrie, Ashville, Ohio

. . . .

19.
Not Haunted Then
Risingsun, Ohio

A lot of people mostly older know my foster parents Bob and Joan. We lived in the Risingsun Bradner area till around 1991. Bob was raised in Risingsun and had lots of family there. Bob's aunt and uncle Joe and Mary Ann owned an inn and the house next to it. In the back of the yard there were a couple of greenhouses. Joe and Mary owned the inn till the time of Joe's death in the early 1970s. I loved that house. It was beautiful and definitely not haunted, but I'm sure I know who might be haunting it.

Around 1971 Joe who had a brain tumor walked out back one night to one of the greenhouses and shot himself. It was a terrible time for the family and aunt Mary had tried leasing out the restaurant, but that didn't work out. She moved to New York with her daughter and family, and the house was sold. I am not sure what might have happened since she moved, but like I said it wasn't haunted when they were living there.

Submitted by Tina, Risingsun, Ohio

. . . .

20.
In The Basement
Mingo Junction, Ohio

I used to live on Lincoln Avenue in Mingo Junction. Not much scares me. The basement always creeped me out a little. I always felt like there was someone down there with me. I figured because it was just dark and gloomy. I decided to finish the back part of the basement and make a man cave. The front part just got too wet. There was also a crawl space at the bottom of the steps. Everything else was good.

Then I kept hearing someone walking around in the kitchen. It wasn't my wife. She was at work, and she worked night shifts. This happened a few times. Then as time went on, I started hearing someone walk down the stairs. I'd run out, and no one was there. I stayed out of the basement for a while after that. After a few weeks I rationalized it and started going back down.

One night I fell asleep, and I heard someone come down the steps. Then it sounded like they were walking around in the next room. I listened scared out of my mind. There was nothing for a while, so I started drifting off to sleep. I heard shuffling next to my chair, and I looked over by where we had a hole and water pump in the corner, and there was this dark shadow. Its eyes were so dark. It seemed like it sucked all the light out of the room. Then I heard evil chuckling, so I ran like I never ran in my life.

In the kitchen I could hear banging and laughing downstairs. I didn't go down there ever again. A year later we sold the house. I did some research a few years after that. The house was owned by this guy who murdered and tortured a couple of women. He was caught and shot by the cops in that very basement.

Submitted by Joe, Mingo Junction, Ohio

. . . .

21.
She Didn't Like Dogs
Grayslake, Illinois

I spent many years of my childhood in a home on W. Belvedere. My great grandfather built the house and the smaller house behind it. The house was definitely occupied by an angry spirit who did not like dogs. Every dog we had while living there died for one reason or another. The house didn't have air conditioning; yet on hot summer days sometimes there would be cold spots around the house. The TV would come on by itself in the middle of the night. My father would unplug it some nights, and we could still hear it come on and turn off.

My mom and one of my brothers witnessed a stuffed animal monkey peek up out of the hamper. Another brother was pushed down the basement stairs, and nobody was near him. When I was nine I slept in a bunk bed on the top bunk. One night I was yanked out of bed by something, and I landed on a black and white television with a broken off antenna slicing open my cheek an inch away from large vein in my neck. I was lucky to only need 14 stitches.

I'm willing to bet that anyone who lived there since late 1970s probably had similar experiences, especially if they owned dogs. I heard stories about car crashes that would happen late at night where death occurred around that guard rail before my time. Maybe related? I still think it was my great aunt who lived in the little house in the back. I understand she wanted the front house when her brother died, but he didn't leave it to her. He left it to my grandfather who rented it to my parents. I don't remember much of my great aunt, but I was told she was very mean and hated dogs.

Submitted by Mark, Grayslake, Illinois

. . . .

22.
Someone In Our House
Alexandria, Indiana

We live on E. Broadway, and there is definitely at least one someone "living" in our house. We have had doors slam when there was no wind. The basement door opened out of nowhere, and we figure it was because someone wanted us to know a leak had sprung down there. We saw a "shadow person" walking in front of our parlor door. I have heard a woman speaking in baby babble to our infant daughter. They were holding a whole conversation with each other on a monitor that we have never had any problems with.

A piece of glass from a broken candle couldn't be found for two weeks. We searched high and low because this is the room our daughter sleeps and plays in. We couldn't find it anywhere. After two weeks of looking one night I went into the kitchen at the opposite end of the house on a whole separate floor, and I found it sitting on the counter. I was home alone, and I know it wasn't there an hour before. Previous homeowners were contacted and confirmed a small portion of similar activity.

Submitted by Jessie, Alexandria, Indiana
. . . .

23.
Friends
Lafayette, Indiana

My daughter and I lived on the south side. There was always activity in the home. It seemed that spirits would come and go whenever they wanted. Most were nice, and I was awakened several times in the middle of the night with a woman shaking my shoulder gently telling me I needed to wake up. I have had my hair played with, and once a little boy crawled in bed with me calling me "mommy." They would annoy my teenage daughter by locking her out of her room and moving her stuff to different rooms.

There was only one dark entity that made us wary of him. He was a tall man, and he would occasionally throw things at my daughter. She has had scratches and marks appear on her out of no where. One night we were discussing my grandparents who had both passed when we watched a glass coke bottle from their home lift off the shelf it was on, and then it was laid down on the kitchen floor. It didn't fall. It was gently placed on the ground. We have since moved, but we enjoyed sharing space with our "friends" as we called them. We sure do miss having them around.

Submitted by Amy, Lafayette, Indiana

. . . .

24.
Voices From Long Ago
Harrison, Michigan

The White Pines Townhomes are allegedly built on an area that was inhabited by the local Indian tribe. The tribe used to summer on the shores of Budd Lake and hunted and fished in the forests and meadows surrounding the lake before they were mowed down by the loggers of the late 18th century.

It is said that during construction of the White Pines Townhomes, bones and other artifacts were dug up, lots of them. Instead of reporting the find to the authorities for the State of Michigan or the Chippewa Tribe, not wanting to stop work while the site was combed over for more relics and remains, the builder threw the bones away and kept right on digging and building.

Now most of the townhome tenants report banging on the walls, lights that flash on and off, and bulbs that burn out quickly. Late at night in the wooded area directly behind White Pines and the grocery store, many people have reported hearing muffled voices and children's laughter.

On one certain night of the year many tenants experience the same paranormal activity: the chanting and drumming of some long ago Native American ceremony. Some have even reported the lingering smell of wood smoke of fires from long-ago. Most of the residents have experienced some type of paranormal activity.

Submitted by Ashleigh, Harrison, Michigan

. . . .

25.
Flowers for The Funeral
Troy, Michigan

I used to live in Troy and in a haunted home. That house was messed up. I personally believe that there was a family in there. My brother and I both saw a man in black. For my brother, he was standing in his room, beckoning him over. For me, he was at the end of a long hallway in the middle of the night. My father saw glimpses of a woman walking through the family room three times.

Since both my brother and I were young, there were toys around the house, which would go off constantly, even if the batteries had been taken out. There is one toy specifically. It was a toy grill, which leads me to believe a fire had run through the home before. Faucets would also turn on randomly, and our television in the family room would turn on every day, on a certain channel at a certain time. If you had been watching some kind of tape or DVD, it would physically kick it out of the player. We still had this TV until a couple of years ago. Once we moved it stopped.

My brother and I also could not breathe in that home when we woke up, which went away as soon as we moved. I also had a disturbing nightmare every single night, from as early as I can remember. In this nightmare there was a small yellow room with a family of Golden Retrievers. Suddenly the room would start violently shaking, as if there was a severe earthquake. After a couple of minutes the shaking would end, leaving the carnage of the dogs. There would be the carcasses of these animals all over the room, much more gore than a young child should know of. This nightmare ended as soon as we moved.

My mother also saw funeral flowers and thought of them as flowers for a child's funeral. She also once was digging behind the fireplace outside and felt as if she was digging up the grave of a child. I do not know of any deaths there, but it was on/in Foxcroft, if you know anything of this.

Submitted by Lillian, Troy, Michigan

. . . .

26.
Thin Veil
Blanchard, Michigan

We were residents in the village of Mecosta for 32 years then moved here to the village of Blanchard 2 years ago. We bought the old mill house next to the mill. It had been for sale for several years. Then it was in foreclosure when we bought it.

We had a new septic drain field and also a metal roof installed by the Amish this year. Our house is a wonderful part of the lumbering history here, and we feel truly blessed to care for it now. Haunted? I'm not sure what's going on here.

I personally saw a young girl apparition one night as I watched TV alone. She had long dark hair and wore a long dress. I left the living room and walked towards the kitchen looking for her, but she was gone!

Also I saw a man walk from the bathroom to the kitchen one night. He also disappeared. My husband was here alone on two occasions and had doors held shut on him. No one was behind the doors either time.

Our daughter saw the shadow of feet moving around in a room upstairs one night. No one was in the room when she looked into it to turn off the light. We had this house blessed twice before moving in. Perhaps the "veil" to the other side is thinner than anyone realizes.

Submitted by Tammy, Blanchard, Michigan

. . . .

27.
First Funeral Home
Evart, Michigan

I moved into an upstairs apartment of a large house converted to three apartments. In the master bedroom you would hear walking and conversations. That was when I started sleeping with the TV on. We found a half door. You had to bend down to walk into this huge room. My kids thought it was great and called it the dungeon. They begged to have that room, so I converted it into a bedroom/den for my kids.

There was a shadow man who was about 9 foot tall. Somewhere there was a picture of him standing behind me in the entrance way of the dungeon as we all came to call that room. Pennies would be tossed in the den. It was nothing harmful, just playful.

I should have known from the first night something wasn't right with that place. I had medicine I needed. It was gone. There were nine people looking for this. We tore apart every room looking for my medicine bottle. The bathroom was trashed from pulling things out of boxes. I became upset. I was in the hallway and was in tears. I said I needed that medicine, and I walked in the bathroom to wash my face. I stopped dead in my tracks. There was a circle in the middle of the floor that was clear. In the middle of that circle standing upright was the bottle of my medicine.

When we moved in to my daughter's bedroom there was an old bed and a small night stand with a bible in it. I disinfected the bed. It was a metal bed with coils that I assumed was made to replace a box spring. I repainted the night stand and put the bible in a closet. My daughter would come out yelling at her brother, "stop crawling under my bed and kicking it and stop calling my name!" Everyone but her was in the living room.

I tossed out everything in that room and bought everything new. I hung rosaries over the head of her bed. I kept her baptism bible she was baptized in wrapped in her blanket in a drawer of the new nightstand.

The apartment directly below me could never keep a tenant. One tenant claimed anything they put on the mantle would go flying off it. Trash cans were knocked over all the time. One of the tenants claimed he looked up the history of the home after they had so many issues, and he found out the building was the first funeral home in town. I never followed up and checked.

We would be awoken at night hearing kids running, laughing, and furniture being moved in the middle of the night downstairs which was impossible. At the time the apartment was empty. You would have doors slam so hard you could feel the floor shake. Whatever was there, it was mischievous. At least for us it was. Downstairs, not so much. I've always wanted to go ask the people living there now if they have ever experienced anything, but I don't want to go back there. Maybe some day I might

Submitted by Anonymous, Evart, Michigan

. . . .

28.
The Same Little Girl
Sturgis, Michigan

About ten years ago I lived in an apartment in Sturgis. My daughter who was three at the time would sit under the table and talk to a little girl. At first I didn't think much about it. I thought it was just a childhood imaginary friend. About a month after that had started she began to tell me the girl's name, what she looked like in detail, and her age.

I started to get creeped out at that point. One night while my girlfriend and I were watching a movie my daughter woke up screaming bloody murder. She came running out of her bedroom saying "she pulled my hair."

My daughter's hair was sticking up a little bit. That night we slept on the couch. My girlfriend had some experience with ghosts in the past and banished her. I had not had any issues after that. When I moved to another unit I was speaking to my new neighbor about it, and she told me she previously lived in that same unit.

She also had the same issues with her son who was also about three at the time. The more we talked, the more we realized it was the same little girl that my daughter had seen. My neighbor gave me the same description of the girl my daughter had given me before I told her anything.

Submitted by Nicole, Sturgis, Michigan

. . . .

29.
From The Closet
Temperance, Michigan

On Crabb Road between Temperance and Substation, there is an old farm house. I will not say the address, as I no longer live there. I did meet an older lady, when I was kid. She used to live in our home when she was a child. She said the house used to have no electricity and that they used candles to see. The house also owned the land from Temperance Road to Dean and Lewis Avenue to Crabb Road. She was a nice lady. She also told us a little bit about the house and where buildings used to be when she was little. Neat history.

Anyways when I was living there it was spooky. The basement was always dark and musty. My brothers and I used to play hide and seek in the dark down there when we first moved in. That was short lived because every time the lights were shut off, something would touch at least one of us, and there was nothing ever there. There was also an old window down there that led to the expanded part of the house. It was boarded up. Kids being kids, we would open it up, and the bravest would go in there to explore on our tummies. My younger brother was chased out of it, and he couldn't tell us what it was. He said it was just a really bad feeling, and he had to get out as fast as he could to escape it. He felt like something was chasing him. I was standing on a chair watching him and also felt the same thing and kept yelling at him to hurry up. I even reached in and grabbed his arms to yank him out.

Our younger brother had felt something bad was going to happen too because when I yanked my other brother out we both fell off the chair to the floor. That was when our other younger brother jumped up on the chair and stuffed the board back in the hole and screamed at us to hurry up and help him. He said it felt like something was trying to push it back out. We both jumped up and ran to help put it back in place. We never went back in there again, and our dad boarded it up permanently. He even got bad feelings from it, he said. It scared us so bad that we refused to go into that area of the basement at all.

I also had my own bedroom, and it had a huge walk in closet with no door. Inside the closet was another smaller closet with a door to the left. You couldn't see it until you walked in there. At night I would hear scratching on that door. It terrified me, and I would refuse to sleep in that room with the door closed unless I had a friend stay the night.

When I was 15 years old my best friend stayed the night with me. At 3:00 a.m. My mom came in and yelled at us to get off the phone and go to sleep, so we did. As soon as we turned off the light, we heard the scratching. My friend looked at me and asked if I heard it. I started laughing and said "thank God, I'm not the only one that hears it". I told her it was coming from the closet. Both of us sat up and looked at the closet where there was no door. As soon as we did, the scratching got loud and really fast like a dog was trying to run on a Pergo floor. Then two huge red slanted eyes appeared in the doorway half way up the door area and growled a growl. We could feel in our chests. You couldn't see into the closet when it happened.

Both of us screamed and fought to get under the blankets to hide, like that was going to work or something. My friend managed to turn the light on just as my mom came blowing through the door to yell at us again. Of course my mom did not believe us, but both of us saw and heard the exact same thing. Scared the hell out of us. My brothers and many of our friends all have many stories from that house. This all took place in 1990 - 2004.

Submitted by Helen, Temperance, Michigan

. . . .

30.
At A "Mom & Pop" Motel
Lancaster, Ohio

I was attending a wedding in Lancaster (I'm from Texas.) Back then the availability of hotels or motels was limited. Not being able to find a room in a newer hotel, I found a room in a little "mom and pop" motel. I wish I could remember the name or what street it was on, but it was not far from the main drag in Lancaster.

At that time I had been skeptic and did not believe in ghosts or the paranormal. My first night there I woke up because it felt like something was pulling the sheets off the bed from the foot end of the bed. I thought I actually saw the sheets move as if someone was at the end of the bed and pulling the sheets with the right hand then the left hand back and forth.

I blew it off to my imagination. I rolled over onto my right side to go back to sleep, and suddenly the bed sunk in on the side like someone sat on the edge of the bed. My body actually rolled toward the side of the bed when it happened.

I was out of there. I slept in my car that night. Then I found a room at another hotel the next day. From that day on I have been sensitive to the paranormal. I see, hear, and feel things all the time. If anyone knows which motel I am talking about, please let me know because I am going back to Lancaster to visit relatives this fall.

Submitted by Martin, Lancaster, Ohio

. . . .

31.
Haunted Home On HWY 46
Deer Park, Wisconsin

Back in 2007 and 2008 my husband and I lived in a house on Hwy 46 in Deer Park, Wisconsin. The house was very haunted. The house had an odd feeling to it, and strange things started to happen right away. There was a pantry in the kitchen, and the pantry door would always open on its own. It happened so often; we finally wedged something against the door to keep it from opening. We had a floor lamp near that door that would always turn itself on. Almost every time I would walk in that room the light would be back on.

Small items in the house would be regularly moved. Footsteps could be heard walking down the hallway almost daily when nobody was there. The bedroom on the northwest corner of the house had a really creepy feel to it. You always felt there was someone watching you, and the TV in that room would turn itself on and off. That was also the coldest room in the house. You never felt like you were alone in that house.

We found out later that the people who lived there previous to us had some friends or relatives living in the basement. The people who lived in the basement would not venture upstairs to use the bathroom when nobody was home up there because they could hear the footsteps moving throughout the house. When I would walk down that hallway at night to use the bathroom, I would always close my eyes because I felt that I was walking through a ghost, and I didn't want to see it.

One time my daughter and I were waiting in the car for my husband, and we saw him come out of the house and come halfway down the outside back stairs only to turn around again and go back up and in the house. When he came back out he was wearing a different shirt. I said "why did you change your shirt?" He wanted to know what I was talking about. He had never gone back up to change his shirt. It was then that we realized we had seen a ghost. I'm sure that place is still haunted.

Submitted by Deb S, Deer Park, Wisconsin

. . . .

32.
Leave Her Alone
Fairmount, Illinois

I had been living in my home for almost two years at the time of my ghostly experience. I have always been interested in the unknown, often visiting areas that are known to be haunted in the area. However, this night in particular was something I will never forget. My boyfriend and I just finished watching one of the paranormal activity movies and decided it was time for bed. We ventured upstairs in my old home to go to sleep. We had been lying there for quite sometime, and I only assumed he had already fallen asleep.

Then it happened. I felt sudden cold breeze, and I felt a heavy force above me. I heard a deep voice loudly say "leave her alone!" At this point I thought I was dreaming and brushed it off. Then my boyfriend said to me in a calm voice as if he thought he was hallucinating, "ummm did you hear that?" I didn't even have to say a word. I got right out of bed and went right outside to my car. He followed, and I did not sleep upstairs for a very long time.

Submitted by Private, Fairmount, Illinois

. . . .

33.
Our White Farmhouse
Preemption, Illinois

I lived in a house a mile and a half south of Preemption
on the left side of the road in a two-story white farm
house. My family lived there for 35 years. In the
summer of 1990 my parents went away to Kentucky. I
stayed home. I had just come home from a friend's
house at 2:30 am and went to my parents' room and got
in bed. I slept in there next to the phone. I had not been
in bed for more than fifteen minutes when above me in
the storage room I heard steady work boots pacing. It
was a very slow pace.

I thought someone was in the house. I very quietly
sneaked out of the house and went back to my friend's
house. I was petrified. The next day I made my friend's
dad check it out. There was no evidence of an intruder.
A few years later a friend of mine who had stayed the
night with me was alone in the house waiting for her
mom to pick her up because I had left for work. She
was in the bathroom getting ready when she looked in
the mirror and saw an old man with a beard staring at
her. She immediately went and sat outside. After these
two happenings there was nothing, but I never felt
comfortable alone again.

In 2007 my mom passed away in the home due to a
massive heart attack. In May of 2017 my father passed

away in a hospice. Two months later a young single father and his four-year-old moved in. In January of 2018 the house caught fire, and the man and son died. The house was a total loss. To date the fire has yet to be explained. My father had five smoke detectors in the house, all of which were going off when fire crews arrived. I never searched the history of the home, but I do know it was well over one hundred years old.

Submitted by Kimberly, Preemption, Illinois

. . . .

34.
Someone Was Angry
Gary, Indiana

Years ago when I was in my 20s I lived in a dumpy apartment complex on 4th Avenue and Connecticut. It has since been torn down and was replaced by a parking lot for the Railcat Stadium. One day while two friends were visiting my husband and me, the four of us experienced activity that until this day I can't explain.

We actually had a large living room in our apartment. Our friends were sitting on our couch as my husband and I shared the loveseat. We had an old 1970s style telephone table directly across the room, far out of reach for any of us. As we were engaged in conversation laughing, I saw the telephone table lift up off of the ground and slam down hard. I saw no one there at all. The best way I can explain it is that it lifted up and slammed down in a way that someone who was angry would do, but visibly there was no one there or even remotely close to it.

I remember looking at my husband and our company and saying "did you guys just see that?" Everyone acknowledged seeing it too. We left the room and never discussed the situation again. I have had feelings all my life, but this instance is the first and only time I have ever seen objects move or anything like that.

My husband and I talk about it every once in awhile. Whenever the subject arises during conversation with whomever and me sharing our experience, I see the looks on faces and feel their disbelief. Although I know it's difficult to believe if you've never had a personal experience, but I stand by what I saw occur that day. First time I ever saw anything paranormal and haven't seen anything like it since.

Submitted by Nicole, Gary, Indiana

. . . .

35.
His Hand Hurts
Adrian, Michigan

When I was very young, still sleeping in a crib, I woke my mother up crying in the middle of the night. She asked what was wrong, and I insisted on getting up and coloring in a coloring book. She finally gave in, most likely so my crying wouldn't wake up the entire household. She set me up at the dinner table with crayons and a book. However, I insisted on two sets of crayons and two books being set up. After doing so she told me to wake her up when I was done or just climb in with her and go back to sleep. Then she returned to bed.

A short while later she got woken back up by the sound of me crying again. She dragged herself back out of bed and returned to check on me. She found me devastated and asked what was wrong, to which I told her that my friend couldn't color with me because his hands hurt. Since she wanted to comfort my tears and I was the only one up besides her at that hour she humored me and asked what's wrong with my friend's hands? I went on to tell her my friend had burned his hands and could not hold the crayons. I went on to describe to her the details of his wounds and that he lived at the end of our street.

At that point she became a bit alarmed. A few years earlier where the small parking lot for Adrian Steel is on James Street by Lansing Street, there used to be some houses, and one of which had caught on fire. While trying to escape the fire a young boy was coming down the stairs and had touched the metal stair rail and burned his hands and sadly died in the fire. It turns out I had described the boy and his wounds exactly. I even told her his name and that he had said that if he would not have touched that rail, he would have made it out of the house safely. I was so sad and just wanted to color with my "friend."

Submitted by Shane, Adrian, Michigan

. . . .

36.
Ghosts Exist
Bay City, Michigan

We bought a house on S Barclay Street that was built in the 1880s. It was foreclosed and empty for about two years. I was alone and painting before moving in, and there was nobody there. I heard a piece of wood drop on the cement floor in the basement, and that scared the daylights out of me. Then as I was painting the living room, I heard coming from the kitchen (mind you nothing moved in yet) noises like what you would hear in a restaurant: dishes and people talking, etc. I finally decided to tell the house out loud that we were there to make the house better and to please not let us hear or see you.

Later I was napping in a chair. I woke up and saw two big black blobs and one little one fly out the window and over the porch roof. Once in a while we hear doors closing upstairs. (We don't use that part of the house now.) I have to have the same talk to not hear or see them. They are cool about it and leave us alone for a while. Not a scary story but still. I believe ghosts exist.

Submitted by Shari, Bay City, Michigan

. . . .

37.
They Are In The House
Pigeon, Michigan

I grew up in an old farmhouse west of Pigeon on M142. My aunt and her family rented the house before my parents bought it, and my cousins who slept in the bedrooms upstairs at the end of the hallway had nightmares every night until they moved out.

When my family and I moved into the house my bedroom was at the end of the hallway. The room across the hall from mine had a weird feeling that made our whole family uneasy. The cat wouldn't even enter that room. Every night I would wake up feeling like someone was staring at me from the doorway of my room. I started leaving the hallway light on at night, and after I would wake up to that eerie feeling I would see shadows moving up and down the hallway. However, I knew no one else was awake, plus the floorboards didn't creak like they did anytime anyone walked across them.

Strange things started to happen all through the house over the course of the next five years. My mom felt a hand touch the back of her head in a comforting manner, but she was sitting in a room by herself in a chair up against a wall. My step dad was walking through the basement and felt someone shove him in the middle of his back, but no one was down there with him. My sisters walked into the living room and saw our mom's rocking chair rocking by itself. My middle sister decided to sit in it to prove her skepticism and felt every hair on her body stand on end. Afterward she began to act very out of character and attempted suicide. My youngest sister said she saw a hand reaching for her from the kitchen ceiling; it scared her so much she refused to be alone in any room for more than a few minutes.

I was home alone one afternoon and kept hearing noises upstairs that sounded like someone was moving furniture around. I knew not to go check it out, so I just ignored it. All of the sudden the door to the stairwell started rattling in its jamb, like someone was banging on it really hard. I left and didn't come back until my mom came home from work.

About a year later I was taking care of my middle sister after she had surgery. I was changing the bandages on her incision, and when I reached for the 4x4 gauze sponge dressing it moved off of the nightstand, hovered in midair for about five seconds, and then slowly landed on the floor like someone gently set it down. It was winter, so none of the windows were open, and the dressing was too heavy for anything to just blow it off the nightstand.

My mom later heard the back story of our house from a local farmer. Back in the 1920s a wealthy farm family owned the property, and their son was engaged to be married. He built the house for his future wife and family and spared no expense. He was paralyzed in a farming accident, and as a result his fiancée left him. His sister moved into the house with him to take care of him and never married or had children. I think our house was haunted by the spirits of the brother and sister who lived there. There must have been a lot of anger and sadness about the events that took place in their lives, and the paranormal events that my family and I witnessed were evidence of that their spirits remained in the house.

Submitted by Ben, Pigeon, Michigan

. . . .

38.

Unwanted Entities

Sault Sainte Marie, Michigan

Last year two of my sorority sisters and I moved into a rental house on the street of Saint James Place. It was a lovely turn-of-the-century home in the heart of downtown. Something always felt a bit off about this place. There was something there with you even if you were the only one home. On occasion strange sounds would echo through the house like somebody had dropped a plank of wood on the floor. We kept finding dead bumblebees all over the basement floor. Most of the activity at this house was small and could easily be dismissed. That was until the three of us returned from a spring break trip.

One of my housemates was out of town for the weekend, but I and the other housemate decided to invite one of our other sisters to stay over. I was in my bedroom when I heard my housemate cry out my name, so I ran out into the hallway to find out what the commotion was about. They were both staring at her bedroom door. One of them told me that the door swung open by itself. Her glasses were also missing. We tore up the whole house looking for her glasses, but they were nowhere to be found.

My attention was drawn toward this one particular shelving unit in her bedroom. I got this nagging feeling that her glasses would be there. We took every item off of it one by one, but they weren't there, so we gave up on the search and decided we would try again in the morning. Later the other two chose to go out to get some fast food, leaving me home alone. I was in my room using my laptop when I heard loud footsteps echoing up the staircase, but there were no creaks. Those steps were impossible to climb without the floors creaking, not even the cat could do it. Worried that somehow an intruder might be in the house, I locked my door and kept a hold of my knife until the other two returned home.

I joined them downstairs in the foyer and warned them that something weird was going on, so they each grabbed an item for self-defense, and we scoured every corner of the building. There were no signs of an intruder. Satisfied that we were the only ones there, we returned to the foyer. My housemate then started joking that it could be a ghost, and we were each making snarky comments, when all of a sudden we heard stomping coming up the basement stairs.

At this point I knew it was definitely something paranormal. Being a witch, I knew how to get rid of unwanted entities. I retrieved the supplies from my room, and we cleansed and sealed the house. Instantly the house felt so much better. The lights in the living room literally looked brighter somehow. We hung out downstairs for a little while before heading to bed. No more weird sounds were heard.

The next morning my housemate told me that as she was settling down to sleep, she felt like something was at her bedroom window. She got up to look, and nothing was there, but she felt this incredible anger just beyond the glass. It was as if something was glaring in at her. When she woke up in the morning, her glasses were sitting on the shelving unit I had pointed out, on top of everything else. We never had an issue for the rest of the year-lease thereafter.

Submitted by Elowen, Sault Sainte Marie, Michigan

. . . .

39.
It Was Probably Floyd
Kingsley, Michigan

When we first moved in to our house (it was an old farmhouse built over 100 years ago) 24 years ago, people would always comment that we moved into the haunted house. At first my mother didn't believe it, until stuff started happening. The thing that convinced her was when she was in the living room, and towels came flying out of the bathroom. Then the cow statue started moving. She has believed the house was haunted ever since.

As for myself, I always felt scared of the basement, like something wanted to harm me. My parents wouldn't say what happened, but we had a priest bless the house. After that we still had some activity, but not negative stuff. An example would be my imaginary friend. One day I had been playing with him, and mom told me to clean my room because we were leaving. I did with her help. When we came back the toys were out again.

We think the spirit here is the first owner, a man named Floyd who died here in a tragic accident involving farm equipment. There are other stories of other owners, but I don't know how credible they are. One of the stories was a couple who took in foster kids, abused them, and one girl died. (Again I can't confirm it.)

Things that still happen here are sightings of a white dog or cat inside the house and shadows of things grown bigger within seconds for no reasons. We have seen a little girl running around outside and laughing a few times. I have had paper thrown at me from the printer that was not plugged in.

Floyd seems to be the one responsible for the pranks because if you tell him to stop, things settle down. We also think Floyd is very protective of children. My sister's first husband moved in, and the house reacted badly.

Some scary stuff happened, for example: banging on the doors when no one was around, cackling, and just some other scary stuff all directed at my sister's husband. We found out later he had a record (as a juvenile) for assaults. As soon as he was out of the house (he did some awful things to my other sister's and was imprisoned) the house calmed down.

Shortly before my nephew was found to be highly allergic to bug bites and the sun, we were hearing knocking on the walls at all hours of the day. When we figured out my nephew was sick, it stopped.

Certain movies make the house act up as well. One time we were going to watch the Exorcist, and my mom put it on the rocking chair. We were the only two in the house at the time, and we both left to get popcorn. When we came back the movie had been moved to the couch, and the chair was rocking. We thought it was weird and put the movie in, and as soon as we did the banging started. We ended up throwing the movie out, and then the house was fine.

Renovations and repairs to the house also seem to increase activity. Again it's mostly banging on the walls, things going missing and appearing days later, and non-harmful stuff. We have also had orbs. I remember being a child and thinking they were fairies, because these orbs hung around my bed at night. After I became a pre-teen it stopped.

Fast forward to my high school years, we finally made the basement nice. It had been a cellar, and so it had dirt floors and stone walls. After we fixed it up, it wasn't too bad. I started having Halloween parties with two or three friends. This one year the prop skull I had started lighting up, which would have been fine, except I hadn't put batteries in it. I was so freaked, so I threw it in the microwave (which was unplugged unless we needed to use it.)

All in all I don't think anything negative is here since we had the house blessed. Whatever or whoever is here seems to be protective and just likes to play jokes.

Submitted by Latsy, Kingsley, Michigan

. . . .

40.
Weird Happenings
Wyoming, Michigan

I grew up by Lamar Park. There was a house on Greenfield that would always have mysterious fires. The residents would also have domestic violence problems after moving there. I knew most of the people that lived there, and they would say flat out it was haunted. Once my friends that lived there and me left that house to play, and somehow a lamp ended up on the bed under the covers and turned on when we came back. (No one else had been in the house.) The bed was just starting on fire when we got there. We put the fire out. However, eventually that house caught on fire again.

I see there is now a new house there. On Wyoming Street my friend died in a mysterious way during a house fire. (He was that same friend.) Another friend told me a big black car with FBI-looking men were following them and asking about what they saw. He said it was really creepy, and they didn't know why these men were following them. A toddler drowned there about a year before, and a woman hanged herself in that garage before that. That whole neighborhood is full of weird happenings.

Submitted by Eva, Wyoming, Michigan

. . . .

41.
Yoo-Hoo
Vestaburg, Michigan

My family lives on the south outskirts of Vestaburg. We bought our two-story stone house in 2007. Before our house fire in 2013, we experienced several unexplained phenomena. I don't recall which was first, but here goes. Once I just finished my shower. I was the only one home. I heard "yoo-hoo." It sounded like my mother calling out to me. I said "I'd be right out. "When I came out to see who was there, my house was empty, and no one was outside either. My two-year old would scream as I laid her back in the bathtub to rinse her hair. I asked what was wrong. She pointed to a ceiling corner and screamed "the tall man!"

Another time my kids were outside playing, and I heard a woman sobbing, but I found no one. My eight-year-old daughter was almost pushed down the stairs by an entity that claimed she was my daughter. My daughter gave a full description of a Chinese girl a year older than herself. My husband claimed to see a light and sometimes a figure in our kitchen while we were all in the living room.

The last entity that freaked me out was during the winter. I went outside to organize my garage around midnight. I was almost finished with my job, using a shop light to illuminate the area with. I looked toward the door and froze as I watched a 3.5' hunched black mass move from outside the doorway out of sight. Our house had been built in 1901, and we found newspapers in the walls from the late 1800s. Ever since we demolished and buried most of the rubble, nothing has happened.

Submitted by Barbara, Vestaburg, Michigan

. . . .

42.
That Man Right There
Petersburg, Michigan

My ex-fiancé and I lived in a brick ranch triplex next to a very old cemetery on Center Street for a couple of years. I have no doubt the place is haunted. We would often hear the pans rattling around in the kitchen cupboards and the floor creaking by the sink. One time my ex, my friend, and I were watching the movie Poltergeist. When it came to the scene with the objects flying around the room, all the lamps and lights in the living room started flickering like mad. We would sometimes hear my daughter who was young at the time talking to someone. When I asked her who she was talking to she said she was playing with the kids. There were no kids that I could see.

One day I came home and my ex said that his hat flew off his tool cabinet on its own and landed right side up on the floor. He also said he saw a young boy. The creepiest thing I saw was one day I was reading while using the bathroom. I kept being disturbed by this crunching noise every few minutes. It sounded like it was coming from the shower, so I opened the curtain and waited to hear the noise again. I literally saw the shower curtain crunch up fiercely at the bottom as if someone were grabbing and crunching it. I ran out of there.

When we were moving out my mom was helping me clean the apartment. She vacuumed my daughter's bedroom. When we went back in, there was a penny lying in the middle of the floor. I picked it up, came back in a little later, and there was another one in the same spot. Then again it happened one more time. We were the only ones there. During the course of living there my daughter would sometimes play with the kids living in the apartment up front. Sometimes I would converse with the mother who told me they previously lived in our apartment before moving into the three-bedroom. She asked me if we had noticed anything "strange" in the apartment. I knew exactly what she meant.

I told her our experiences, and she told me about how her kids had a remote control car that kept driving around on its own. They thought it had a short, so she removed the batteries and put it on the table. The car drove off table with no batteries. She had music boxes that would just start playing at random times. She said her son was talking to someone one day. When she asked who, he said "that man right there! Don't you see him?" I am curious to hear what others who have lived there have experienced.

Submitted by Anonymous, Petersburg, Michigan

. . . .

43.
Occupied
Carrollton, Ohio

I lived in a home on E Shannon Avenue in West Carrollton OH from 1977-1998. During that time I have seen and heard things in that house that still can't be explained. I remember as a child waking one night, and on my bedroom closet door was a face of a man that was slowly coming out of the door. I screamed for my mom to help me.

As soon as I did, it was gone. As a teen I was up late one night, so I decided to make a PB&J sandwich. I was standing in the kitchen, and it felt as if someone was standing right behind me. I turned around, and no one was there. I went back to fixing my sandwich, and immediately that feeling returned. When I said "thanks for offering, but I can handle this myself," that feeling disappeared.

Another time my sister and mom had gone out shopping, leaving my dad and me there watching TV. All of a sudden we both heard a sound like someone was upstairs in the full house length attic, throwing wooden boards from one end of the attic to the other and back. This lasted about two minutes. When it stopped I grabbed a flashlight and stood at the bottom of the stairs looking up the staircase. No one was there, and nothing was out of place. When we moved from there the people that moved in after us only stayed there for a couple of months. The man had told my dad that they couldn't take the strange feelings and noises any longer. The house is still there currently occupied.

Submitted by Don, Carrollton, Ohio

. . . .

44.
A Girl Scout
Western Springs, Illinois

I used to work at a company in Westmont, IL. During my lunch breaks I would go to Bemis Woods in Western Springs, IL to walk through the forest preserve. I would park at Dean Nature Sanctuary and take the trail through Bemis Woods to a parking lot in the middle, and then I would walk back to my car.

One sunny warm day I was walking the trail going back to my car when I encountered a girl, walking the same trail towards me. She was about 9-10 years old and was wearing a black dress almost down to her ankles. As we passed each other, I said hi, and she said hi back. I found it unusual that such a young girl was walking through the forest preserve all by herself and that she was wearing a dress that looked like something a girl would wear in the 1920s or 1930s. Other than those two things, nothing else was unusual about her.

After I came home, the thought came to me that maybe the girl I saw was a ghost because of the dress she was wearing. I searched the internet for "ghost of Bemis Woods" but found nothing.

Today, which is a few years after I saw the girl, I typed "girl ghost of Bemis Woods" again to see if anyone else has seen her. A link came up to a website stating that there was once a Girls Scout cabin in Bemis Woods in the 1920s. Girl scouts would meet there from 1921 to 1925, and later the cabin was destroyed. No one knows today where it was located exactly, but the general location where they believe it was located was where I saw the young girl that day. I now wonder if the girl I saw was a Girl scout who used to spend time at that cabin.

Submitted by Tom, Western Springs, Illinois

. . . .

45.
Rural Highland
Highland, Illinois

Highland is definitely a paranormal "hotspot". UFO's have been sighted there several times, and I myself saw one in the backyard of our residence on Laurel Street back in 1969. My neighbor saw it also. My good friend's father was chased into a ditch by one while working on his farm in rural Highland. Seeing as Ghostsofamerica concentrates mainly on Ghosts I've got a dandy story for you.

It involves the same friend whose father had the experience with the UFO. I won't disclose his name, but I've known him since we were kids back in the sixties. When he and his wife first got married (1986) they moved into the small house on his father's farm in rural Highland. After a couple of kids that house became too small, so sometime in the early nineties they moved into town on Main Street about a block away from the hospital. I should mention, at this point, that the elderly couple that they bought the house from had not wanted to sell it but were forced to for financial reasons.

Many times my friend would tell me stories of how this couple would just show up at their door unannounced asking if they could once again walk through the house that they loved so much. My friend, being a nice guy would always let them even though, after several times, it began to get weird. On one of these occasions the old man stated that he planned on "moving back into the house" when he died! My buddy shrugged it off as nonsense until the old couple passed away. Everything was business as usual for the first few years. However, one day my friend and his wife decided to remodel the kitchen. Big mistake!

Almost immediately strange things started to happen. This is going to seem unbelievable, but I swear it's all true. This house began to rival the Amityville horror. The first event happened in their hot tub just off the back porch. They had been throwing a small gathering when suddenly one of their daughters' boyfriends came in from the hot tub. (He had been out there alone.) He was pale as a ghost. When they asked him what was wrong. He described seeing a tall female specter who appeared out of nowhere and started to walk towards him. After that things just got stranger and stranger.

Voices could be heard (and were recorded). A constant static crackling noise could often be heard moving throughout the house. There were shadows seen marching up and down the hallway at night. The family dog would stare into the air and follow something as it moved around the living room. One of his daughters experienced so many terrifying things that she refused to sleep in her bedroom any longer. There were a group of nuns who lived in the house

102

next door. They also began having strange occurrences in the one room in their house that was closest to my friend's daughter's room (just a few feet way). The nuns eventually moved away stating that they could not take it anymore.

Various psychics, mediums, and local ghost hunters were brought in to try to help. One of these psychics told my friend that there was a large portal in the basement where various entities were coming through. When the ghost hunters were brought in, they were actually able to interact with one of the spirits in the daughter's bedroom. They tied a tennis ball to a string and hung it from the ceiling. Upon command the entity would start swinging the ball. They also did many EVP (electronic voice phenomenon) sessions and caught some great recordings.

My friend identified one of the reoccurring voices as that of the old man he purchased the house from. Evidently he was the spirit who was moving the tennis ball. One night when he refused to move the ball he was heard on the recording stating that there were "too many damn people in here. " I swear some of the recordings they got were the best I've ever heard. At one point they were walking around the backyard with the recorder and caught the sounds of a military platoon marching through the yard. The recording is crystal clear, and you can hear everything from marching feet to the clanking of metal.

We assumed at first that this was a residual sound from the Civil War, but when we checked it out we could find no records of military activity around Highland during those years. However, I dug a little deeper and discovered that there were lots of military troops in the area around Highland during the War of 1812. Eventually all the activity just faded away, but it all went on for several years. The house has been quiet now for about eight years or so. I spent the night in that house about ten years ago and witnessed many of these strange occurrences for myself and heard these unbelievable recordings. This entire experience was a real strain on my friend and his family, but being an avid fan of the paranormal, I found it to be utterly fascinating. I have no doubt that this house was one of the most active examples of the paranormal that I have ever heard of bar none.

Submitted by Mark, Highland, Illinois

. . . .

46.
A Pure Sees Things
Bourbon, Indiana

We moved in our house three years ago. Our house was built in 1887 I do believe. I personally have never seen a thing but only heard things such as footsteps with floor creeping, stuff hitting the wall, and mumbling. I can never make out what they are trying to say. I do recall one or two times I was asleep in the middle of the night.

Then someone was saying my name close to my ear really softly. It freaked me out, and I woke up instantly and looked around. All I could think is "What the hell? Please tell me I am just crazy." You know how people say if you are pure you will see? Well if you haven't, that's what people say.

I do have a pure, and she is now four. She has told me horrific detailed description of some she has seen. She came to me one day said "mommy, there are two dead men hanging in the bathroom." I thought "holy ----. There is no way she made that up." Another incident happened when I was giving the girls a bath. My oldest again said "mom? I just saw daddy walk through the kitchen." I said looking around, "baby, daddy is not here." That was completely utterly weird, and it creeped me out.

My daughter also talks about a hand trying to get her and balls her eyes out because she is scared. It just got brought up last night again as she ran into the bathroom crying to her dad because the hand was going to get her. If it gets any worse, we are moving.

Submitted by Ashley, Bourbon, Indiana

. . . .

47.
An Old Southern Gentleman
Manchester, Michigan

I was driving through Manchester on M52 very early morning. It happened to be pouring rain. There was only one other car in sight. I went through the stop sign and was driving past the funeral home. Out of nowhere a man appeared walking on the sidewalk in front of the home. I know he had not been a second before. All I could see was his back.

He was dressed in a white suit with a white straw hat, and he was using a walking cane. He was very much like an old southern gentleman. It definitely caught my eye because I don't expect to see someone taking a strolling walk there at 5:30 am in the middle of a downpour and he was definitely not dressed in present day attire. He looked very much out of place.

I was moving forward and was trying to get a look at his face as I was passing him. As I was about to pass, he literally vanished in thin air in front of my eyes. I was so startled. I almost went off the road. At that same time the other car that that on the other side of the road squealed his car as he slammed on his brakes. I looked at him, and he was looking in the same place the man was and had vanished.

He had the same look of "what the hell was that!" that I am sure I had on my face. I knew I wasn't alone, and he had seen the man too. I don't know what we saw that morning, but I know I won't forget it.

Submitted by Katherine, Manchester, Michigan

. . . .

48.
The Women
Harrison Township, Michigan

I moved up here from Florida into an apartment on Jefferson with a lake view. One day I was sitting in my apartment when I saw this woman walking by my apartment, and she peered into my window. I went outside to ask her what she was doing. I had told her that someone lives in that apartment. She stated that she too had lived there 30 years ago. She was a very beautiful woman and was young in age.

The woman said that the apartment that I lived in used to be a two-story with the bedroom upstairs. She also stated that the lake water was very close to the apartment which is not the case now. She came up from the lake and was wearing very tall black waterproof boots. She was very kind and sweet, and then as suddenly as she had appeared, she disappeared.

On another occasion I was going to my car on a very cold winter morning, and another woman very soft spoken and quiet appeared in front of me. I said "good morning" a few times before she responded, and then very softly she said "good morning. " She stated that she was going to inside and clean the hall of the apartment, and then she too suddenly disappeared.

Now I see some kind of a smoky figure move across the room, and my cat gets on all fours and stares. You are probably wondering why I still live there. The reason is because they are not harmful to me, and I do not believe they will hurt me.

Submitted by Samantha, Harrison Township, Michigan

. . . .

49.
Full Of Spirits
Flint, Michigan

I grew up in Flint. When I was two my dad got a job at the V8 Engine plant, so we moved from Ohio to an upper floor apartment on E Page Street. It was a beautiful home built by hand by the downstairs occupants Mr. and Mrs. Lerdrop. All the wood embossed paneling was sent over from Denmark. Upstairs in my room was a huge walk in closet. I was terrified of it. Something lived in it. There were sounds of scratching and bumping around.

When I was five the elderly couple had both passed away, and we moved downstairs. My bedroom opened into the dining room (where all night I could hear people talking and furniture moving.) The other door opened into a short hallway with the bathroom (and my parents' room in the back.)

One night I was brushing my teeth, and I happened to look over at the doorway. There, I saw a very thin pale arm stretching across the entire door frame! I looked away and looked back. It was still there. I started to walk over to look closer, but it disappeared. That house was full of spirits!

Submitted by Anita, Flint, Michigan

. . . .

50.
Walking With Me
Gwinn, Michigan

I lived on Mustang. The first night I moved in I heard someone running up and down the stairs. I thought my kids were up, but when I went to check they were sound asleep in bed, and no one else was there. From then on it got worse. I started hearing someone calling my name, but being a skeptic I always looked for logical reasons. Then I started getting touched. Then weird noises and footsteps increased. Everyone in my home started noticing these things. We all started having nightmares and seeing weird shadows moving.

One night I was walking down the stairs, and I instantly felt really cold, and my husband looked up at me. He looked freaked out. He said he saw a little girl with dark brown hair walking down the stairs with me. I saw a cigarette moved 180 degrees around in an ashtray. One night I woke up to what sounded like a party in my room. I opened my eyes, and my room was full of blue, white, and gold orbs. As I reached over to wake my husband the noises and the orbs disappeared. I moved a few months later and have never experienced anything like that since.

Submitted by Does not matter, Gwinn, Michigan

. . . .

51.
He Was So Sorry
Seville, Ohio

My daughter and son-in-law bought a house in Seville in 2013. It had been all remodeled, and they got it for a good price. My daughter gave birth to their first child around six months later. She said she always felt sad in the house and could feel spirits there. I did some investigating and found out that a man had taken his life there not long before. I found photos of him and so forth. I told my daughter, but she never wanted to see his pictures.

One night while watching TV in her room, she took a selfie and threw the phone because there was a man's face in the photo behind her. She described him to me, and I thought it sounded just like that photo. I showed her, and she almost started crying. She said he didn't scare her. She just felt his sadness. Often she would see shadows on the baby video monitor. It was as if someone was looking at the baby.

We had someone come in with paranormal equipment, and she felt a very strong presence. She also barely screwed on Maglight flash lights that we opened and put new batteries in. Then she asked him questions. He would flash the light once for no and twice for yes. He was most definitely present. We had another person come in, and she didn't know the back story. She immediately began to cry. She said he was so sad, he wanted his family, and he was sorry for doing what he did. She then said he was happy there was a new family and he wanted to stay. She told him it was time to go. After that there wasn't a lot of activity, just occasional visits.

Submitted by Anonymous, Seville, Ohio

. . . .

52.
A Gold Orb
Waterford, Michigan

I used to live in a subdivision off of Hatchery Road in Waterford. One night I let my dog outside to do her business, and she started walking down the sidewalk sniffing the ground like she picked up a scent trail. She got about halfway past the neighbors' front yard before I caught her and picked her up. I was about halfway up from bending down to pick her up when I felt something very big and very fast fly right over my head. It felt the wind when it went past my head. It moved my hair.

I thought it might have been an owl or something, so I looked in the direction it was heading toward, and I saw a gold orb about the size of a basketball hovering approximately ten feet above the middle of the street. I stared at it for a few moments, and it slowly faded out of sight. I looked at my dog who I was holding, and she was staring at the same spot where the orb had just disappeared. We went back in the house as fast as we could.

Submitted by BC, Waterford, Michigan

. . . .

53.
Was It the Old Landlord?
Danville, Illinois

We lived in a converted apartment house on the corner of Hazel and Penn Streets in 2014 Danville in Illinois. Not too long after we moved in we could hear someone walking up and down the stairs to the top apartment no one lived in yet. The kids were afraid of the kitchen even in daylight. They said the backdoor handle would shake. Sometimes it would sound like dishes crashing, but nothing fell. I would see shadow figure across shower curtain while showering. I came home from work, and sometimes my door would be wide open when I knew I shut and locked it. A couple of times I came home, and the radio was on full blast.

Over time things escalated. Our toys started turning on by themselves. The kids said stuffed animals flew across the bedroom. They even claimed to see ashtray on table move. At bedtime we felt uneasy, and something sounded like whispers in our ears. This takes the cake; one night when my boyfriend and I were up watching TV we thought we heard one of the kids out of bed. He said he went to bed, looked toward the hall, and saw a head of hair poking from around the corner. We checked on the kids, and they were asleep.

We actually think we captured a photo of a dark headed woman peering through the dining room window. It was a full apparition with facial features and all. We moved eventually, not due to haunt but financial reason. We moved just across the street. Sometimes the lights blink on an off over there, and I can see it. It could very well be haunted. The landlord said the lady that used to own it was dying of cancer but didn't die in the house, but she's buried right over in Spring Hill cemetery.

Submitted by Anonymous, Danville, Illinois

. . . .

54.
Weeping Spirit
Harrison Township, Michigan

I used to fish down by the lake in Harrison township by Middle School south of the cutoff road by the park. There is a wall with the words El Paul on it. Then after the walkway entrance wall there is a field. I rode my bike there one day, and on the big boulder concrete rock was a 20-year old looking female wearing all black and black shoes. I stood and stared for two minutes because it looked as if she was curled in a ball with her head in her arms crying, but I could not hear her cry. Her back was moving like a person crying would.

This looked like a human, but what was weird was that I rode my bike there and stared and a normal human would look up since we are curious beings. Well, all she did was keep her head down. I talked to a wiccan, and I was told that more than likely what I saw was a powerful spirit. I've seen shadow people, and I'm not crazy. I work at psychiatric wards, and I am a nurse here in Vegas now. However, since I was told it is a spirit I actually do believe that. This was an early-20s-girl wearing a lot of black sitting on a rock that I like to sit on while fishing. It's very crazy!!!

Submitted by Justin, Harrison Township, Michigan

. . . .

55.
Apartment 3
Edgerton, Wisconsin

I lived in a place on N Main Street Apartment 3. A few different things happened while I lived there. The first thing happened the day I got my key after signing the lease. I went in and did a walk through to see what needed cleaned before moving my possessions in. While I was in the kitchen pantry I heard in a woman's voice yell ''Hello'' from the other end of the apartment.

Thinking one of the neighbors came through the front door to greet me, I walked to the living room, and no one was there and the door was locked. At all times of the day you can hear what sounded like someone walking down the hallway.

The second super scary thing happened while my cousin and I were hanging out in my room searching the internet. Then out of nowhere from right outside my bedroom door we both heard a man whistle. The hairs stood straight up on both our arms and instant chills.

Another time my cousin Mike and I were watching a movie in my room. I was lying in bed, and he was sitting in a chair across the room from me. We had eaten popcorn, so I grabbed some floss and then set the floss container on my dresser. I got back in bed; a minute later the floss went flying across the room and hit Mike in the head.

Submitted by Danielle, Edgerton, Wisconsin

. . . .

56.
She Came Home With Me
Carpentersville, Illinois

I live in Carpentersville, IL right near the Carpentersville dam. I am the last house on our street, and the forest preserve is my back yard. There is a gravel trail that runs along side my house that leads into some more dirt trails that allow a person much more access around the woods. I frequently visit the forest during the day but mostly at night because it gives off a certain energy that I'm drawn to.

Well, I've braved walking the dirt trails alone at night with myself and my cell phone used to guide my way. Last year I had my brother and a friend walk with me late one night through the Raceway Forest Preserve, aka my backyard. I like to just point my cell phone in any direction while walking in the darkened forest while video recording.

After an hour of walking with my brother and friend hoping we'd see some strange phenomena, we went back to my house where I watched my videos closely. Then my friend pointed out in two of the videos what seemed to look like a woman walking next to us at two certain points of the video.

I definitely knew there was no one else with us then, so it wasn't a living person. You could see her legs going in a walking motion in the video, but all you could see was from her knees up. The grass wasn't high enough to have covered her feet up to her knees. It was crazy seeing this on video. It gave my brother, our friend, and myself chills. Also in the video in a slow motion voice we heard "go home" in the background.

Ever since that night I've had numerous strange things happening in my house, from my ceiling fan turning on by itself to my dresser drawer opening by itself. I also had inanimate objects being flung across the room, and one time one falling right into my hand while I was sleeping, which woke me up. I felt the spirit of this woman followed me back home where she made her presence known every so often. The latest incident was while I was brushing my teeth, and the fan for the air vent turned on by itself.

Submitted by Blanco, Carpentersville, Illinois

. . . .

57.
Evil Spirit
Portsmouth, Ohio

I know for a fact that the house on 17th Street in Portsmouth, Ohio is haunted, and it is not a nice entity either. I lived there for five years with my five kids and my husband. I was never really sure what I believed in before this house, but I know there is an evil presence there. There are also other spirits there, but it seems the evil spirit is more active although my son often saw shadow people. One in particular was a small boy and his dog. My daughter was born the last year that we lived there, and then he began to see a very tall dark shadow of a man in a hat stand over me while I slept by the baby's crib. My son claimed to even see it pick up the baby one night.

I put it off as a vivid imagination for a long time, but then others felt and saw things also including myself. I always felt that someone was trying to push me down the steps. I never dared to stand at the top ever, and I didn't let my children either. My children would not sleep upstairs, nor would they go up there by themselves. We heard people walking upstairs. We constantly heard music playing and humming. We have seen numerous sights of shadows and unexplained occurrences in that house, and I always felt an eerie feeling of that evil . The house was built in 1923, and this seems to be all the info I can find on the house. My mother, her boyfriend, and my three nephews lived in the house a year after we moved, and they couldn't wait to get out of the house either.

Submitted by Barb, Portsmouth, Ohio

. . . .

58.
The 700 Block
Greensburg, Indiana

When we lived on East Washington Street in the 700 block. I was five years old, and I was in bed sleeping when I heard a noise of scuffling feet coming down our hallway. I looked at the curtain that was our door, and two hands pulled the curtain open. In walked a robot looking creature, and I closed my eyes.

Then another night the same thing happened. I closed my eyes, and then I opened them when the scuffling noise stopped. I saw two large red eyes looking at me. They were maybe one foot away. I closed my eyes and froze there. I heard chanting, and I was scared to death.

Then another day I woke up, and I had a big goose egg bump on the side of my head. I showed mom, and she gave me this story. My dad stopped the next door neighbor from taking me out through the bedroom window. My dad must have hit me while trying to stop the neighbor.

This house was haunted, I know. My big brother took a plastic ball bat to bed with him one night. It was the same room where me and three of my brothers slept. That night he felt the bat being pulled from his hands, and in the morning it was broke in half. This all happened while we lived there. We moved when I was six years old, and all those things stopped where we moved to.

Submitted by Paul, Greensburg, Indiana

. . . .

59.
Tragedy After Tragedy
Brighton, Michigan

We live on Lake Moraine. Since moving here in about 1998 the entire subdivision has been struck by tragedy after tragedy. Shortly before I moved in, a high school girl across the street committed suicide. My neighbor's high school son died in a car accident. The boyfriend of a resident killed himself. My next door neighbors were involved in a murder-suicide.

There have been nearly a dozen neighbors involved in car accidents, four of which suffered various sorts of brain damage. Four weeks apart two high school boys were in separate car accidents. They were both residents of the subdivision. In each case they were one of four passengers, and each was the only survivor.

One neighbor reported that, after moving into their home, they found a room in the basement. The entire room was painted red and contained a crib. They immediately had the room blessed and repainted it. A couple of months later they received some sort of underground satanic magazine. It was not the type you could ever purchase in the store, but rather a homemade version. The family that reported this has got to be the most honest group of people I've ever met.

I myself have been witness to many supernatural events in my own home. Both of my children, as toddlers, would point at a fan or a mobile, and it would begin to spin. If they looked away, it would abruptly stop. Eyes glow golden in the mirrors.

I once entered my parents' bedroom and said goodnight to my mother. I could see the outline of her on the bed. She groaned and rolled over. I then went into the living room. About five minutes later, my sister and mom showed up. Nobody was in the bedroom.

Last summer in the basement I encountered a being. Unlike whatever that creeps the neighborhood, this being was benign. Perhaps it was even friendly. It was almost like a mirage consistency, about my height, and clearly with the shape of a human. I approached. What surprised me most was that, as I walked near or through the being, it was warm. It was not cold as I would expect.

I've tried to research the area but have come into many difficulties. I asked that anyone with similar stories please share them, especially in this neighborhood.

Submitted by Mikaela, Brighton, Michigan

. . . .

60.
The Other Residents
Stevens Point, Wisconsin

I don't have any photos sadly, but until I was about six I lived in a two-story little white house on Portage Street just a few houses from the river and a few houses away from West Street. I lived with my sister, my mom, and my dad. We also had multiple other "residents." The others that I can specifically recall was Bobby, Bobby's brother, the upstairs grandma (Bobby and his brother's mother,) Henry, and the lady in the window. Bobby and his family used to live in the house before my family lived there.

There were also a few other "residents" in the basement, but I chose never to go down there. I constantly saw the spirits every day, and I would constantly talk and play with them. They would constantly turn the water on and change the temperature of the house. My parents were skeptical when I was young and just thought that it was my imagination until stuff happened to them, like doors shutting, windows opening on occasion.

We weren't the only people in the neighborhood who knew there were spirits who lived with us. Growing up my mom always worked second shift (2 pm-11 pm,) and my neighbor asked my dad why my mom sat in the window from 8 pm until about 11 pm. That's the first real encounter my dad had because he knew that my mom didn't get home till about 11p m. I constantly remember sitting in my bedroom just talking to the spirits in my bedroom.

Submitted by Alicia, Stevens Point, Wisconsin

. . . .

61.
Black Mass
Chicago, Illinois

In Lakeview or Boystown (W Melrose Avenue near the lake) there is a haunted apartment building. I did not believe in the paranormal before I lived here. I saw a 7-foot-tall deep black mass one night, and when I tried to get a better look at it (because I could not believe my eyes) it rushed at me. It was a terrifying moment. For weeks after I thought I was losing my mind. Then my husband saw a black mass moving through the apartment. I knew it wasn't just me. I saw the entity a couple more times, but it was never as large or threatening.

The apartment always felt dark to me, and I often felt like we were being watched, but I played it off easily. We later moved to a very old coach house in Humboldt Park, and that place felt much warmer and more homely to me.

Years after we moved out I did research on the address and did not uncover any deaths. I also messaged the property management and asked if they've ever had tenants complain or report paranormal-type incidents. They confirmed they had, so I was not alone!

Submitted by HC, Chicago, Illinois

. . . .